Series 654

Acknowledgments
The publishers gratefully acknowledge assistance provided by
L. J. Carter FBIS, Executive Secretary of the British Interplanetary
Society, in compiling this book; and also the use of photographs as
follows: page 43 (top) British Tourist Authority; page 51
Nassa/Space Frontiers.

HOW IT WORKS...
THE ROCKET

by DAVID CAREY
with illustrations by
B. H. ROBINSON

Ladybird Books Loughborough

Introduction

Space travel is often in the news. Many films and stories have been written around this intensely interesting subject, but none of these captured our attention more than the actual facts of man's historic landing on the Moon on 20th July 1969. His successful escape from the Moon's gravitational pull and subsequent safe return to Earth were equally stirring.

Space stories we see on the screen or read in books are sometimes based on fact, but the imagination of the authors is used to add fiction to fact and make the tales as exciting as possible. But what really happens when a rocket is launched? How is it propelled? How does it travel in the emptiness of space? Why do space vehicles stay in orbit around the Earth when their store of propellent has been used up? These and many other fascinating questions are answered in the following pages of this book. Not all rockets are used as space vehicles—several other uses are also described.

There are two other Ladybird books which will provide more information for boys and girls of all ages who have an interest in aeronautics and astronautics. These are: 'How it works—The Aeroplane' and 'Exploring Space'. The aeroplane has an entirely different set of problems to overcome in comparison with the rocket, as you will see. 'Exploring Space' tells the story of man's achievement in space and the great progress being made towards learning more about the Universe in which we live.

But first, how *does* a rocket work?

Rockets made possible man's first Moon-landing

Rockets versus Aircraft

Aeroplanes rely for their operation on the atmosphere which surrounds the Earth. They are driven forward by forcing the air backward with their propellers, or with the exhaust gases from their engines in the case of jet aircraft. The air acting on their wings gives them lift, air pressure is used for turning and banking, and oxygen from the air enables their engines to work.

Air is at its greatest density at sea level. As height increases the density becomes less. Five miles up, that is about the height of Mount Everest, the air is only one quarter as dense as it is at sea level. For an aeroplane this means that there is less air to push backward for forward motion, less lift for the wings and less oxygen for the engines. At twenty miles above the Earth an aeroplane reaches its absolute ceiling because there is just not enough air for it to operate. It is obvious, therefore, that no aeroplane will ever fly in space, let alone reach the Moon.

This brings us to the essential difference between the aeroplane and the rocket. Rockets do not need air. They travel better above the atmosphere where the air is so thin it offers little drag or resistance to forward and upward motion. The oxygen needed to operate the rocket's motor is carried in a tank built into the rocket itself. Once the Earth's gravitational pull has been overcome the rocket will continue on its chosen path without further propulsion.

The limitations of an aircraft compared with a rocket

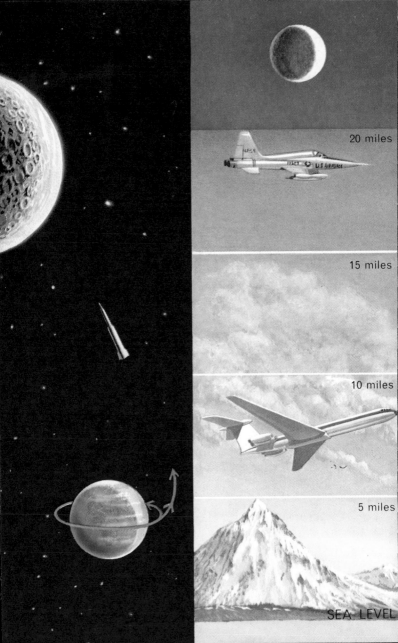

20 miles

15 miles

10 miles

5 miles

SEA LEVEL

First Principles of Rocket Propulsion

When you walk upstairs you do so by pushing *down* with your foot on each step. When you climb a rope or a tree you lift your body upward by pulling *downward* with your hands. In fact, to move in any direction you have to exert pressure in the opposite direction. The movement in the one direction is exactly equal to the pressure in the other. To express this principle in its correct form we say that "To every action there is an equal and opposite reaction." (*Newton's Third Law of Motion.*)

When a rifle or any sort of gun is fired, there is a sharp recoil, or kick-back, after firing. This is the backward reaction of the gun to the forward action of the bullet or shell leaving the barrel at high speed.

Now, if the gun were pointed toward the ground and fired, the recoil would be in an upward direction. That is very roughly how a rocket works except that, instead of a bullet leaving a barrel, we have a stream of hot gases leaving through a downward-pointing exhaust. The kick-back from these gases ejected at very high speed reacts toward the nose of the rocket and propels it upward. A gun recoils once after each bullet is fired, but, because there is a continuous stream of gases leaving the lower end of a rocket, it is forced upward in a continuous motion.

An aeroplane is propelled forward by pushing back the air. A rocket does not push back air to go forward; its movement is caused by the action and reaction of the expanding gases in its combustion chamber.

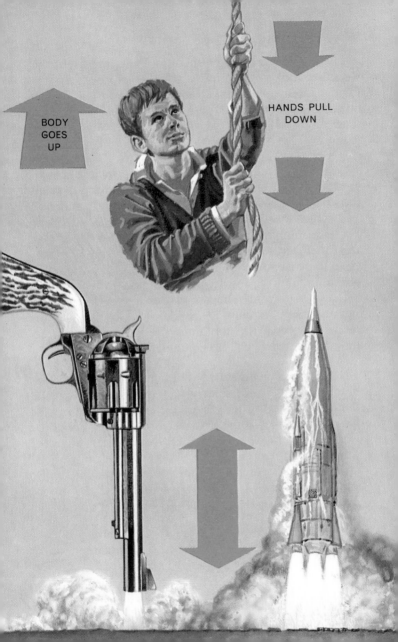

BODY GOES UP

HANDS PULL DOWN

Why it Works

The principle of rocket operation is so important that we must look into it more closely before going any further. Remember that a rocket does not go upward by pushing air downward. Its upward movement is the reaction to a downward force provided by escaping gases.

A simple explanation of the reaction principle appears in the diagram on the opposite page. The top drawing shows a spherical container, like a hollow metal ball, into which propellents have been injected and burnt. These burning propellents, or combustion gases as they are called, are intensely hot, with the result that they expand at an enormous rate. By doing so, they exert pressure all round the inside of the container. There is no outlet through which the gases can escape so the pressure, or force they produce is spread equally all over the inside surface of the container. Because all the forces are equally balanced the container does not move.

Now, if we include an exhaust in the lower portion of the container and fold back the edges of the metal (lower drawing), the gases will escape through the opening and the balance of the forces in the container will be upset. The gases will escape freely through the exhaust and the upper portion will have an unbalanced upward force which will therefore move the entire container upward. This upward force is equal to the force of the gases escaping downward through the opening.

In a rocket there is a combustion chamber which works in just the same way as the open-ended container.

A diagram of the reaction principle of a rocket

Propellent Storage Tanks

It has now been clearly established that a rocket's upward or forward motion is made possible by hot exhaust gases escaping at high speed through the opening at the rear. These gases are created by burning special propellents inside the rocket. Large tanks are built into the rocket to carry the propellents; in fact these tanks are the largest parts in the rocket's structure and the weight of propellent they contain is often as much as ninety per cent of the weight of the whole vehicle before it is launched. It is therefore necessary to use the kind of propellents that will give the greatest thrust for their weight and the amount of space they take up. In other words, they must be as efficient as possible.

Similarly, the tanks themselves must provide maximum capacity with minimum weight. A thin rocket will create less drag than a fat one as it travels up through the Earth's atmosphere, so the tanks must take up as little sideways space as possible. To save unnecessary weight, the tank sides have to be very thin. This means that a strong material is required.

Some types of tank are built separately and then fitted into the rocket tube. Another kind is built as part of the main structure, the sides of the rocket actually forming part of the tank. This design saves weight because the one section of material does two jobs. Tanks are sometimes made to fit round the outside of the rocket so that they can be jettisoned when they are empty and their useless weight does not have to be carried any higher than necessary.

An illustration of a Rombus rocket with jettisonable tanks, and a diagram of a fuel tank fitted into a rocket tube

FUEL

Types of Propellent

Every internal combustion engine needs oxygen to ignite the fuel which provides the power. Motor car and aeroplane engines operate in the atmosphere from which their oxygen supply is drawn, but rockets travel above the atmosphere, where no oxygen exists and they must therefore carry their own supply with them.

Most large rockets are of the bi-propellent type. This means that they employ two separate fluids, each stored in a different tank. One of the fluids is an oxidant which provides the source of oxygen the fuel needs to make it burn. The other fluid is the fuel itself which burns in the oxygen and releases energy in the form of hot gases which flow at high speed from the combustion chamber. (Remember our open-ended container on page 10.)

The oxidant is usually carried in the form of liquid oxygen, nitric acid or hydrogen peroxide. Liquid oxygen is an obvious choice but the other two fluids also have a high oxygen content.

The fuel must burn efficiently to provide the highest possible exhaust velocity, because the speed at which the exhaust gases leave the combustion chamber determines the rocket's upward thrust. The more efficient the burning, or combustion, the greater the exhaust velocity, and the greater the thrust. Kerosene (paraffin) is the most commonly used fuel at present but the lighter and more energetic liquid hydrogen is gradually replacing it.

Solid fuels are sometimes used. These have the ability to be stored, without evaporating, but are not quite so powerful.

A Redstone rocket with Mercury spacecraft

FUEL

OXIDANT

The Propellent Pumps

From the previous chapter we know that most large rockets use two liquid propellents, each stored in a separate tank. But before the rocket can function, these propellents have to be fed into the combustion chamber and ignited.

The first items in the fuel feed system are the pumps. These are located below the tanks and their job is to pump the propellents from the tanks, through control valves and injectors, into the combustion chamber. A pump consists of a bladed wheel, known as a turbine, which is driven by chemically-produced, high-temperature steam. It is mounted between two turbo-impellers. These are metal discs fitted with blades or vanes. We have all swished water round the bath with our hands to get the hot or cold water circulating quickly. When we do this, our hands are acting as impellers.

The steam is directed at the turbine blades, thus causing the turbine wheel to revolve. This in turn rotates the impellers. As they rotate they draw the two propellents from the tanks and push them along pipes towards the combustion chamber. One of the impellers pumps the oxidant while the other pumps the fuel. Great care must be taken to ensure that the two fluids do not come in contact with each other in the pumps, otherwise there could be an explosion and the whole rocket would be destroyed.

Rockets consume vast quantities of propellents at an enormous rate, so the pump impellers must be capable of rotating at very high speeds to keep the supply flowing.

A Rocketdyne F.I. America's largest liquid-propelled engine

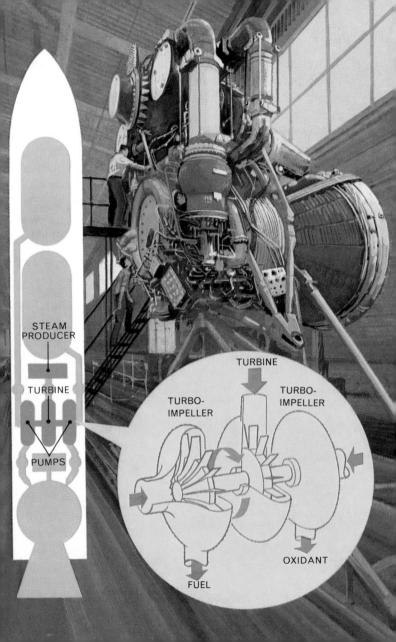

STEAM
PRODUCER

TURBINE

PUMPS

TURBINE

TURBO-
IMPELLER

TURBO-
IMPELLER

FUEL

OXIDANT

Valves and Injectors

Valves are inserted at various points throughout the rocket's propellent system, to control the flow of fluid from the tanks to the pumps and then on to the combustion chamber. They also regulate the movement of the steam which operates the turbine pump. Besides this, they are used to obtain the correct direction and quantity of flow of the liquids which pass through them. They open to allow the fluid, steam or whatever it is to pass along the pipe and close automatically when the required amount has gone through. The incorrect functioning of any one of the many valves could cause the complete destruction of the rocket.

Injectors are the last items in the rocket's propellent system. They are fitted to the combustion chamber casing and have very fine nozzles which protrude into the interior of the chamber. The oxidant and fuel are fed into separate injectors and, as they are forced through the nozzles, the fluids are converted into a fine spray of tiny droplets. If you have ever used one of the many household atomisers and seen the fine, misty spray that comes out of the small hole at the top, you will have a good idea of the effect produced by the injector nozzles in a rocket.

Rocket injectors have to be designed so that the atomising and mixing of the oxidant with the fuel in the combustion chamber are as complete as possible and produce a vapour mixture that will burn with maximum efficiency.

Testing under conditions of extreme cold

VALVES

INJECTORS

Combustion Chambers and Igniters

The combustion chamber has already been mentioned several times. It is the most important part of the rocket motor because it is here that the thrust which drives the rocket is finally produced. All the systems and parts described have just one purpose, that is, to get the propellents into the combustion chamber where they can be mixed and burnt in sufficient quantity to provide the downward exhaust pressure that will force the rocket upwards at high speed.

Some fuels and oxidants will ignite, or burn, of their own accord when they are forced through the injector nozzles and mixed together. That is why great care has to be taken to keep them apart in other sections of the rocket. However, most of the propellent mixtures require a source of heat to ignite the vapour in the combustion chamber.

Igniters are used for this purpose. There are various types in use, one of which is the spark plug type (as in the motor car). This is mainly used for small rocket motors. Then there is the 'firework' type, rather like a Catherine Wheel mounted on a stick attached to the launching platform. Another kind of igniter is in the form of a miniature combustion chamber connected to the main chamber. In this the fuel/oxidant mixture is ignited by a spark and the resulting explosion ignites the bulk of the mixture in the main combustion chamber.

20

IGNITER

COMBUSTION
CHAMBER

Cooling the Combustion Chamber

It is difficult for us to appreciate the great heat that is generated in a combustion chamber when the propellent mixture is being burnt. The temperature of boiling water is one hundred degrees Centigrade and we normally consider this to be quite hot. But the combustion chamber of a rocket can reach as much as three thousand degrees Centigrade, or nearly five thousand, five hundred degrees Fahrenheit, at the point of burning.

This intense heat creates problems for rocket designers because the chamber has to be made of metal, and this has to be as thin as possible to save weight. As no known metals will stand anything like three thousand degrees Centigrade without melting, some means of cooling the combustion chamber wall must be found otherwise it would simply melt away and disappear.

Various cooling systems have been used but the most efficient method employs a double wall all round the chamber, with a space between the two layers of metal. A cooling liquid is then introduced and circulated within the space to absorb some of the heat of the inner wall which is in direct contact with the burning gases. The system operates in the same way as the water jackets in a car engine. (See 'How it works—The Motor Car'.)

The cooling fluid is nearly always the fuel, which is circulated as the coolant before then being injected into the combustion chamber and burnt.

This double-wall system is known as regenerative cooling.

A Saturn rocket under construction

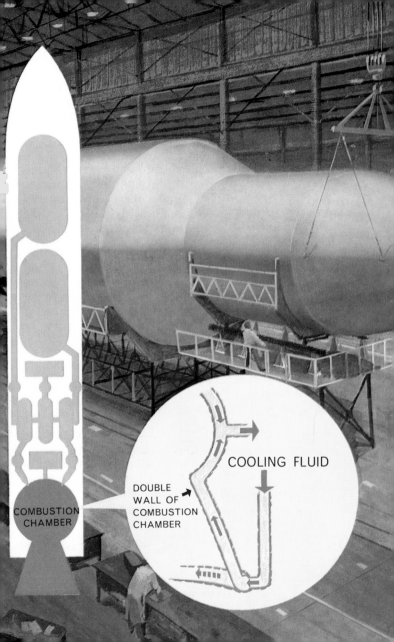

COMBUSTION
CHAMBER

DOUBLE
WALL OF
COMBUSTION
CHAMBER

COOLING FLUID

How a Rocket Motor Works

So far we have dealt with the principles of rocket operation and the various components which go to make up the complete rocket motor. In this chapter we will see how each individual part does its job and how the whole firing operation is started and made to function continuously.

1. The valves controlling the flow of the fuel and oxidant from their tanks are opened and the two liquids begin to flow downward through the connecting pipes. They flow freely under the natural force of gravity through other open valves leading to the pumps and injectors, and then pass to the combustion chamber.

2. The fuel and oxidant mixture is ignited in the combustion chamber and produces an initial thrust. Because the pumps are not yet working to force the propellents through the system, this initial thrust is only of low power and is not sufficient to move the rocket off the ground.

3. The chemicals which provide the steam to operate the pump turbine are now allowed to come together by the opening of other valves. Steam is produced and the pump impellers start turning.

4. With the pumps in operation, the propellents are pushed through the system in greater quantities and at greater speed. They spray through the injectors with greater force until a stage is reached when the downward exhaust pressure is sufficient to produce the thrust necessary to blast the rocket into the air at an ever-increasing speed.

The actual operating sequence of a rocket is therefore quite simple.

Different kinds of Rockets

In this great and exciting age of space, it is very natural to think of a rocket only as a vehicle which carries the astronauts up through the atmosphere and sends them, in their spacecraft, hurtling toward the Moon at about twenty-five thousand miles an hour. This is the rocket's most glamorous and most exciting role. But in considering the rocket as a whole we must not forget its many other functions.

First, of course, there are the little rockets which adults and children enjoy launching every year on November the fifth—Guy Fawkes night. This is a far cry from sending men into space but the toy rocket was the start of the whole business. Rockets such as these use a small quantity of solid fuel which is ignited by lighting the blue touch-paper at the lower end. The fuel burns very quickly and in doing so creates a downward pressure which sends the rocket surging into the air. The stick attached to the fuel container is simply to give the rocket directional stability and prevent it from toppling over and flying off in the wrong direction.

Some aircraft are fitted with booster rockets. These help fighter aircraft to get off the ground quickly, and boost their rate of climb so that they reach their operational height in as short a time as possible. They also assist heavily-laden aircraft to take off from airports with short runways, and aircraft at relatively high altitudes where the lift from the air is reduced.

An F.104G Starfighter—an aircraft which is assisted on take-off by a solid fuel rocket

More Rockets

Rockets can be used to rescue people from ships in trouble. Equipment is set up either on the shore or on another ship and a small rocket carrying a thin rope, or life-line, is fired across to the vessel in distress. The life-saving gear is then hauled aboard and the rescue is carried out by 'breeches buoy'. Many thousands of lives have been saved by this method which has been in regular use around the coast of Britain for nearly a hundred years. Small ships in difficulties, themselves sometimes fire distress rockets to attract attention.

Then we have the less peaceful application of the rocket. Missiles, as they are called, are used against various targets in wartime. There are ground-to-ground missiles fired by troops at targets on the ground. The German V2 rocket of the last war was one of the first examples of this type. Ground-to-air missiles are used in an anti-aircraft role, and air-to-air missiles are fired from one aircraft at another. From these we go onto the air-to-ground missiles released from aircraft onto ground targets. There are also anti-missile missiles which are designed to intercept other missiles on their way to a target.

All these missiles are forms of rocket, working on the same principles as we have described earlier in this book. They vary in size and have special instruments which guide them on to their targets, but their motors function as rocket motors.

Bloodhound ground-to-air missiles which have wrap-round rockets

Ground Stations

All round the world is a series of stations which receive and process information from satellites and space probes, and frequently control the space mission.

The American manned spaceflight network, for example, consists of thirteen regular stations, with tracking and support ships as required, to provide continuous contact between the ground and the space capsule. The accuracy of these stations is amazing. One radar, for example, can fix the location of a capsule to within seven yards at a distance of five hundred miles.

Ground stations really carry out four different services:

Tracking, i.e. continuously reporting the position of the satellite or space probe. Location is very important and must be related to a particular time; position is necessary so that commands may be sent to make observations, transmit data, or change the flight path.

Telemetry. This converts information into signals to be received by ground stations and then decoded again. Radio telemetry can describe everything from an astronaut's blood pressure and heartbeat to the strength of the Earth's magnetic field.

Control. The ability to direct a spacecraft by means of a network of ground stations. Some information must be gathered and acted upon instantly, e.g. in manned space flight. Other data is required merely so that one station can inform the next of an orbital pass.

Command. Which means using a ground station radio transmitter to send signals to make a satellite operate in a certain way, e.g. to start or stop a camera, change direction or fire a rocket.

A view of a control room at Cape Kennedy

Payload

The nose cone contains the payload. This is most important for it is the reason for which the rocket has been constructed and launched.

The payload is what the rocket, or any other form of transport, is built to carry. A motor car carries people; trucks carry goods; trains, ships and aeroplanes carry passengers and freight. The people, the goods, the passengers and freight are the payloads of their respective vehicles.

Rockets are used for a variety of purposes, so their payloads differ. The payload of a missile is an explosive warhead, that of a research vehicle is scientific instruments or a complete artificial satellite. Perhaps the most exciting payload of all is a space capsule to send astronauts into orbit round the Earth or heading for the Moon.

Of all the forms of load-carrying transport, the rocket is the most expensive, mainly because it is required to generate enormous thrust to overcome the pull of the Earth's gravity, and also because it can be used only once. By comparison, forms of transport on Earth are much more economic. For example a little Mini car will carry four people, a truck weighing two tons will carry three tons of goods, and all other forms of transport will carry a high percentage of payload in proportion to their own weight. But a space rocket is usually thirty to forty times as heavy at launching as the payload it carries. This is chiefly due to the tremendous amount of propellent it has to take with it to keep the motors working. Of course, the further it goes, the lighter it becomes as the propellent is progressively used up.

A U.S.A.F. manned orbital laboratory

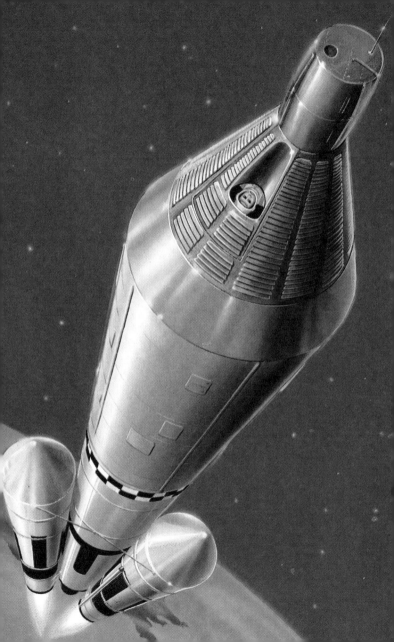

The Force of Gravity

Having now discovered how a rocket works and what it is for, we can go on to other aspects of rocket operation. So let us consider some of the outside forces that must be overcome before we can leave the ground and get into space.

Why do things normally stay on the ground anyway? When we fall down, why do we fall *down*? If you throw a ball into the air it always comes back to Earth—why? The answer is—'Because of the force of gravity'. We stay on the ground because the Earth's gravity holds us down; we fall down because the Earth's gravity pulls us down. The same applies to the ball—it does not just drop back to Earth, it is pulled back by gravity. All bodies have gravitational pull, the greater the mass, or amount of material in the body, the greater the pull. Because the Earth is so much more massive than anything on it, everything else is pulled towards the Earth's centre. We fall down because we cannot pull the Earth up.

There are two ways of overcoming gravity, at least for a time; by exerting an upward force greater than the force of gravity—*lifting* a ball into the air; by speed—the harder you *throw* the ball the faster it goes and the greater the height it will reach. (1 & 2).

Resistance caused by the Earth's atmosphere is another force acting against a rocket. The efficiency of a rocket is greatly increased in the absence of atmosphere.

How the pull of gravity decreases with distance from the Earth's centre (3)

8,000 miles from earth's centre

12,000 miles

16,000 miles

g $\frac{1}{4}$ g $\frac{1}{9}$ g $\frac{1}{16}$ g

① ② ③

Escaping from the Earth

The Earth's gravitational pull is something we live with all the time, we take it for granted and hardly ever think about it. But it is a most important factor in rocket operation and must be overcome if we are to get anywhere in space, or off the ground at all.

The example of the ball, already given, holds the secret. The harder the ball is thrown, the faster and higher it will go. The secret, then, is speed. If we could throw the ball hard enough it would go up and up forever and never come down. The speed at which it would have to be thrown to do this is known as 'escape velocity'. Of course, we cannot *throw* a ball hard enough because the speed required to escape completely from the Earth's gravity is seven miles per second, or over twenty-five thousand miles per hour.

Once escape velocity has been reached by a spacecraft, no further power is needed. A rocket aimed at the Moon, for instance, will 'coast' the rest of the way because the Earth's gravity cannot then pull it back, and there is no air resistance in space to slow it down. This 'coasting' is known as 'free fall'. That does not mean the rocket is falling down towards the Earth but that it is travelling freely in space without the aid of power, like a bicycle coasting downhill.

Free fall is an important feature of space travel: it would be impossible to carry enough propellent to provide powered flight all the time.

Principle of the Step-Rocket

In rocketry, one problem very often leads on to another. Having determined that a speed of twenty-five thousand miles per hour is necessary to escape from the Earth, the next problem is how to achieve it. With the propellents at present in use it is not possible for a single rocket to reach this speed. Gravity and the resistance caused by the atmosphere are too strong. Scientists have therefore devised a method of attaching two or three rockets together, one above the other, and these are known as step-rockets.

What happens is this: the bottom rocket carries the other two plus the payload, and provides the power for the first stage of the flight. When its propellent is exhausted, the motor of the second rocket is started, and the first rocket separates and falls away to get rid of its now useless weight. This means that the second stage starts with the advantage of speed and height provided by the first. When the propellent of the second rocket is used up, the third rocket's motor starts and the second stage separates. We are now left with one rocket plus payload, its speed and height boosted by stages one and two. By the time the propellent in stage three is exhausted, escape velocity has been reached and the payload is in a condition of free fall and can orbit or go on into outer space—to the Moon if desired—without any further assistance.

In the illustration, the second stage propellents are shown as being forced into the combustion chamber by the use of compressed gas, instead of by pumps as used for the first stage. The third stage is shown as a solid propellent rocket.

How the step-rocket works

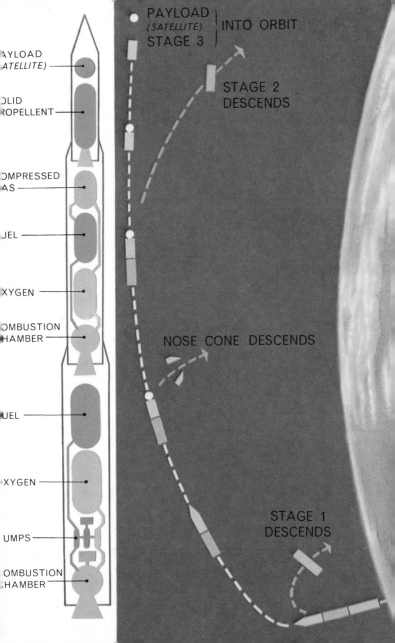

PAYLOAD
(SATELLITE)

SOLID
PROPELLENT

COMPRESSED
GAS

FUEL

OXYGEN

COMBUSTION
CHAMBER

FUEL

OXYGEN

PUMPS

COMBUSTION
CHAMBER

PAYLOAD
(SATELLITE)
STAGE 3 } INTO ORBIT

STAGE 2
DESCENDS

NOSE CONE DESCENDS

STAGE 1
DESCENDS

Problems of the Step-Rocket

On page thirty-two, dealing with the payload, it was said that rockets could be thirty to forty times heavier than the payload they lift off the ground. This applies mainly to step-rockets, in which the first stage lifts not only the final payload but stages two and three as well. And, of course, each rocket can only be used once. If we take the mighty Saturn V rocket, for example, we find that, at launching, a weight of nearly three thousand tons is required to place a one hundred ton payload into an orbit around the Earth, send forty-five tons to the Moon, or thirty-five tons to a planet. For single-stage rockets, the ratio is not so high.

Another problem is to secure the various stages together. The fixing bolts have to be strong enough to hold the system together and resist the stresses, strains and vibrations set up during flight. They must also be capable of being broken when required so that the stages can separate. Separation itself is a problem. It has to be exactly timed to coincide with the using up of the propellent in one rocket and the firing of the motor in the next.

One method of separating one rocket from another is to use hollow fixing bolts. A small explosive charge is put into the hollow bolts and at the right time the charges are set off by means of an electric signal. This shatters the bolts and allows the spent rocket to fall away.

Into Orbit around the Earth

Because it is very expensive to launch an artificial satellite or spacecraft, scientists obtain the utmost value from them once they are launched. Many of the research projects carried out by space vehicles need a considerable time to complete, and it is essential that all the scientific instruments operate efficiently for fairly long periods.

Most of the satellites launched to date have been put into orbit about two hundred miles above the Earth's surface. This distance varies because the orbital path is rarely a true circle but an ellipse. Now, two hundred miles is still well within the most powerful part of the Earth's gravitational field. How then, can we keep a satellite from being pulled back to Earth although it is within the Earth's gravitational field? The answer, once again, is speed.

Attach a weight to a piece of string. Hold the loose end of the string and swing the weight in circles above your head. So long as you are swinging it fast enough the weight will maintain a path horizontal to the ground. Slow down the swinging movement and the weight will fall. This shows again, that given enough speed, the force of gravity can be beaten.

A speed of twenty-five thousand miles per hour is required to escape from the Earth altogether, but eighteen thousand miles per hour is sufficient to maintain an orbital path at a height of two hundred miles, for here the orbit of the satellite is curved to the same extent as the Earth's surface, and the satellite, in effect 'falls' round the Earth. The higher we go, the less speed is required as the force of gravity becomes weaker.

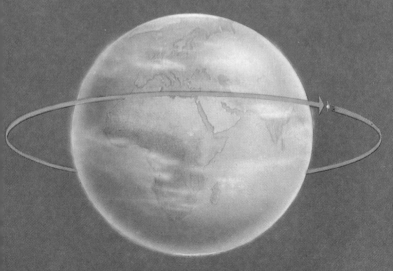

Movement in Space

Even with to-day's expert and precise methods of launching, a rocket or space vehicle could still go off course. It is therefore necessary to have some means of steering the vehicle so that its flight path can be corrected from time to time.

A ship can be steered because its rudder acts against the water through which it is travelling. The direction of an aeroplane is controlled by means of air pressure against its rudder. A car relies on the pressure of its tyres on the road and it will go in the direction in which the front wheels are turned. In space there is no air and no pressure; nothing of any kind for a steering system to get a grip on. So we come back to the reaction principle. Just as a rocket reacts upward to a downward force provided by its motor, so the same principle is employed to turn a space vehicle in any other direction.

Little rockets or compressed air nozzles are fitted at suitable points in the space vehicle. When a change of course or attitude is required the appropriate rocket is fired in a short burst. This pushes the vehicle toward the opposite direction and thus alters the direction of flight.

The same procedure can be used to slow down a space vehicle for re-entry into the Earth's atmosphere or for landing on an airless body like our Moon.

Orbiting manned capsules contain retro-rockets at their base. The base of the capsule is positioned to face the Earth on re-entry and the rockets fired, the capsule's final descent being undertaken by parachute.

The procedure is identical for a lunar landing, except that the parachute is not needed.

Tracking Satellites

Even the largest artificial satellites placed in orbit around the Earth are very small when considered against the background of space. Sometimes they can be seen as tiny pinpoints of light moving across the sky. More frequently, special telescopes are needed to pick them out. But sight requires a clear view and if the sky is cloudy nothing can be seen.

Keeping in contact with, and tracking a satellite is frequently done by radio. The satellite is provided with a radio transmitter to send out signals, usually information it has obtained from its instruments, and these can be picked up by receiving sets on the ground. But if the transmitter fails to work, or its batteries become discharged, no signals will be sent out and the usefulness of the satellite is over.

Another method of tracking is by the use of radio telescopes. Just as an ordinary telescope collects light waves, so a radio telescope picks up radio waves. A great deal of information can be gained in this way even though no visible picture is produced. A radio telescope can also be used as a radar device to measure distance and so calculate orbits. In this method a 'pulse' is sent out which bounces back off the satellite and is recorded on instruments attached to the telescope.

A world-famous radio telescope is at Jodrell Bank in Cheshire. It has a wire 'saucer', two hundred and fifty feet in diameter, which can pick up radio waves from far out in space. Many similar radio telescopes exist in other parts of the world to provide a comprehensive tracking and control system for deep space-probe rockets.

A radio-telescope

Messages from Space

Each artificial satellite is placed in orbit for a specific purpose. Sometimes this is purely scientific, such as measuring cosmic rays from outer space or radiation from the sun, or observing the stars from above the Earth's obscuring atmosphere. Other satellites have some practical everyday purpose, such as help in navigation, radio and T.V. relay, mapping the Earth or in studying the Earth's weather.

The transmission of information from satellite to Earth is done by a system known as telemetry. It involves the use of a special kind of radio transmitter using radio waves in the v.h.f. (very high frequency), u.h.f. (ultra high frequency) or s.h.f. (super high frequency) ranges. Normal radio waves are not able to penetrate the Earth's atmosphere but are absorbed or reflected back to the transmitter by the 'ionosphere', a layer of ionised gases which lies between thirty and seventy miles above the Earth's surface. It requires radio waves of very great penetrating power to get through this barrier.

Power for the satellite's telemetry and other instruments is often provided by solar cells. These make use of the fact that sunlight, falling on special plates made of silicon material, generates an electric current. Whereas small electrical storage batteries become exhausted very quickly, solar cells can operate for a long time and so greatly prolong the useful life of the satellite and the amount of information it can transmit.

The End of the Beginning

No book on rockets and space travel can ever be finished. In past centuries man has explored the Earth and has found much to wonder at. The Moon, the planets and the stars have been studied from the ground and a vast amount of information has been gathered— some of it right and, as it turns out, some of it wrong. The study of space *from* space is our latest adventure. A great deal has been learned in a few short years but we are still only scratching at the door that will one day open and lead us to the conquest of the Universe. This may lie centuries ahead, but it will surely come.

All these high adventures will depend on the rocket for their beginnings. Propellents will undoubtedly change and be made more efficient; atomic energy or electrical propulsion may well be used, but until such time as we can use solar energy as a means of propulsion, the general principles of rocketry will continue to apply.

Radio signals, received over millions of miles have been translated into visible pictures of the surface of Mars. New radio telescopes will soon be able to send commands and to receive information from space probes as far away as Pluto which is three thousand, six hundred million miles away and the most distant planet known. Man has already set foot on the Moon; one day he will also tread the surface of Mars. And this will be just the beginning.

Part of the desert on Mars, as seen by the Viking 2 Lander, part of which can be seen in the foreground

Short Glossary

Astronautics—*The science of travel in space, including problems of artificial satellites and space probes.*

Attitude Control—*A system to turn and maintain a space-craft in the proper direction.*

Boost—*Extra power given to a rocket during lift-off, or in flight, e.g. with a booster rocket.*

Bi-Propellent Rocket—*A rocket in which the fuel and oxygen are fed separately into the combustion chamber.*

Capsule—*The top or instrumented stage of a space vehicle.*

Circular Velocity—*A speed needed to maintain a satellite in a given circular orbit.*

Combustion Chamber—*The chamber in a rocket where the fuel and oxident are united and burned. It also includes the nozzle.*

Control Rockets—*Small rockets used to control the attitude or slightly change the speed of a spacecraft.*

Cosmonaut—*The Russian term for an astronaut, i.e. space-traveller.*

Count-Down—*The count, in inverse order, of the hours, minutes and finally the seconds of the time remaining before the launch of a rocket (there is also a* count-up*).*

Escape Velocity—*The speed needed to escape from a given point in a gravitational field. This speed, at the Earth's surface, is 6.95 miles per second.*

Fuel Cell—*A cell in which a chemical reaction is used to produce electricity.*